A
Tool

A resource for people with an interest in
scripture, students-of-scripture, college
students, believers, and clergy

Thomas Williams, PhD

A Tool

Thomas Williams, PhD

Copyright © 2015 Thomas Williams

Published by 1st World Publishing
P.O. Box 2211, Fairfield, Iowa 52556
tel: 641-209-5000 • fax: 866-440-5234
web: www.1stworldpublishing.com

First Edition

LCCN: 2016900612
Softcover ISBN: 978-1-4218-3748-2
Hardcover ISBN: 978-1-4218-3749-9
eBook ISBN: 978-1-4218-3750-5

This material has been written and published for educational purposes to enhance one's well-being. In regard to health issues, the information is not intended as a substitute for appropriate care and advice from health professionals, nor does it equate to the assumption of medical or any other form of liability on the part of the publisher or author. The publisher and author shall have neither liability nor responsibility to any person or entity with respect to loss, damages, or injury claimed to be caused directly or indirectly by any information in this book.

Foreword

Writing "A *Tool*" was a challenge and daunting process. The devil fought me but I kept writing, praying, and trusting the Lord. I thank and praise the Lord Jesus Christ for taking me through this process.

A *Tool* can be used as a study guide, a Sunday school book, a training tool, a discipleship training manual, and as an academic textbook, a resource for a Bible study as well as a resource in a cell group. Depending on your needs, decide how you want to use it.

Acknowledgements

I thank and praise the Lord Jesus Christ of Nazareth for how He encouraged me through the love, support, and prayers of my precious mother, Dr. Alice Williams; my precious brothers and sisters: Charlie Jr., Alicia Ann, Jimmy Lee, Daniel, Denise Rice, the late Leonard Aaron, and David Williams; a dear friend and faithful brother, Bishop Kurt Dawson; my son-in-the-faith, Pastor Chadwicke Cannon, Sr.; one of my Daytona Beach, Florida mothers, Dr. Christine Wallace Davis; a precious colleague and dear friend, Mrs. Audrey Lea Anderson Biggs; and my precious brother, friend, and mentor in the academy, Dr. Anthony T. Woart.

World without end,

Thomas Williams

Thomas Williams, PhD
Bluefield, West Virginia
October 27, 2011 (original statement)
October 21, 2013 (revised statement)

Christian author Dr. Thomas Williams is a product of the Newark, New Jersey public school system. Williams holds two doctorates and is a licensed and ordained minister. Thomas Williams lives and works in Bluefield, West Virginia and is the author of 2 in 1 (released by 1st World Publishing). Dr. Williams and can be reached at drthomaswilliams79@yahoo.com.

A *Tool* is a thought-piece grounded in scripture and inspired by the Holy Ghost. The views expressed therein were NOT endorsed or underwritten by any denomination or educational institution and are thus solely those of the author.

In loving memory of Charlie Mack Williams, Beanie Mae Wilson Brown, Bishop Dr. Carey Cornish Bowles, Leonard Aaron Williams, Rosa Sarah Wilson Bowles, and Helen Curtis Suggs—a few people who I miss and still love

To the people of God who operate in the spirit of the
great commission and reproduce spiritually

"The voice of one crying in the wilderness, Prepare ye the way of the Lord, make his paths straight"

—(Isaiah 40:3).

Scripture Quotations

I am not a King James-only person and thus use other translations to help bring another voice and fresh face to the text. Not unless otherwise indicated, scripture quotations are from the KJV, 1611 edition.

Scripture quotations are also taken from the following English Bible translations:

BRUCE HUMPHRIES, INC. AND CHICAGO MOODY PRESS: Scripture quotations marked (Williams) are taken from The New Testament in the Language of The People by Charles B. Williams copyright ©1937, by BRUCE HUMPHRIES, INC. Copyright renewed © 1965 by Edith S. Williams Chicago Moody Press 1963.

CONCORDIA PUBLISHING HOUSE: Scripture marked as (Beck) are taken from The New Testament in the Language of Today by William Beck © 1963 Concordia Publishing House, St. Louis, Missouri.

CROSSWAY BIBLES: The Holy Bible, English Standard Version (ESV). Copyright @ 2001 by Crossway Bibles, a division of Good News Publication of Wheaton, IL. Used by permission.

HARPER AND ROW PUBLISHING, INCORPORATED: Scripture quotations marked (Moffatt) are taken from A New Translation of the Bible Containing the Old and New Testament. Concordance Edition

Abbreviations

Beck – The New Testament in the Language of Today

ESV – English Standard Version

Howard – Hebrew Gospel of Matthew

KJV – King James Version

Moffatt – A New Translation of The Bible

NAB – New American Bible

NASB – New American Standard Bible

NIV – New International Version

NKJV – New King James Version

NT – New Testament

OT – Old Testament

Phillips – The New Testament in Modern English Second Edition

Sterns – Jewish New Testament

Williams – The New Testament in the Language of The People

Using "A Tool"

I respectfully offer the following suggestions as a guide for using *A Tool*:

- Decide how you want to use A Tool in light of what you want to teach and get across to your students (disciples).
- Use scripture but do NOT choke your audience to death with them.
- "Use biblical history but not at the expensive of, nor in place of scripture" (Williams, 2011, p.19).
- Use words and scriptures in context.
- Self-disclose when appropriate but do not make the class just about you and your experience.
- Be humble and always be ready to hear from the Lord and your audience.
- Do not put any person, group, and or denomination down.
- Encourage and guide your audience into answering their own questions.
- Be flexible
- Always remember that" humility carries the day" (Williams, 2011, p.165).

TABLE OF CONTENT

CHAPTER 1

A Snapshot into the Ministries of Three Key Historical Figures:
Moses, Jesus Christ of Nazareth, and Saul/Paul of Tarsus

Introduction

Each of the three historical figures plays a powerful role in the history of the world. For instance, Moses represents the law (John 1:17), whereas Jesus Christ of Nazareth is the Savior of the world (Acts 13:23), the prophet that would come (Deuteronomy 18:18-19) as well as the desire of all nations (Haggai 2:7). Saul of Tarsus, on the other hand, according to Williams (2011), "hated and tried to destroy the fledging (young) Jewish congregation" (p.87) but "the Lord watched Paul and stopped him in his tracks and used him [Saul/Paul] to turn the world upside down" (88). In this three section chapter, a snap shot will be presented of the ministries of Moses, Jesus Christ of Nazareth, and Saul of Tarsus. For our purposes, a snap shot is a brief (quick) summary of a few key points about a person's ministry.

Chapter 1, Section 1
A Snapshot into the Ministry of Moses

Moses was from the tribe of Levi (Exodus 6:20) and is the key figure in the Pentateuch (first five books in the O.T.). When Moses was born, Israel was in bondage (slavery) in Egypt, and he was born a slave.

History notes that Moses went from the house of bondage to royalty but never forgot his roots and people. For instance, "one day, he [Moses] saw an Egyptian mistreat a Hebrew and [Moses] killed him [the Egyptian]" (Williams, 2011, p.25). When the pharaoh learned that Moses had killed an Egyptian, the pharaoh wanted his life (Exod.2:15). To avoid sudden death, Moses left Egypt in a huff and went into Midian (Exod. 2:15).

When Moses lived in Midian, he got married, became a father, and a shepherd (Exodus 2: 21-22). Being a shepherd probably helped Moses to become the leader that God wanted him to be.

Moses spent approximately forty years in Midian until God called and sent him back to Egypt when he was approximately eighty years old (Exodus 3:7-10) to tell pharaoh to let his people go (Exod. 7-14-15; 8:20-21; 9:13-14, NIV). According to Freeman (1996, p.15), "pharaoh is a common title of the native kings of Egypt and was given to [him] because he was considered the representative [vicar] of the sun god." While in office, the pharaoh was considered to be the ruler of Egypt and a god, who owned his "subjects" and the land (Lawrence, 1991, p. 429).

Moses had several admirable characteristics. For instance, he was a friend of God (Exodus 33:11), very humble (Numbers 12:2, 7, NIV) and a faithful servant (Hebrews 3:1-2).

A Snap Shot into the ministry of Moses:

- To fulfill prophecy (Genesis 12-13);
- To be a servant (Hebrews.3:1);
- To be a deliverer (Exodus 3:10);
- To be a ruler (Acts 7:35);
- To be a leader
- To spoke for the Lord God (Exodus 9:1);
- To be obedient (Exodus 7:10);
- To prophecy (Deuteronomy 34:10);
- To give the law (John 1:17);
- To teach the law (Deuteronomy 4:44);
- To enforce the law (Num. 15:32-36);
- To intercede for Israel (Exodus 15:23-25);
- To be a military leader (Exodus 17:1-13;
- To establish a court system (Exodus 18:21-26);
- To serve as Israel's first chief justice (Exodus 18:26); and
- To establish tribal elders (Numbers 11:16-30).

Summary

God raised Moses up from humble beginnings and used him to lead Israel in the desert for approximately forty years. Although he was meek and had a close relationship with God, Moses did not go into the promise land because of disobedience.

Thought

Older people should serve as leaders in the church.

Chapter 1, Section 2
A Snapshot into the Ministry of
Jesus Christ of Nazareth

Introduction

God never intended for the gospel to be limited to just one nation but made it available to all men through Abraham (Genesis 12:1-3) when God sent Yeshua into the world to die for our sins according to the scriptures (1st Corinthians 15:3-4).

About Yeshua of Nazareth

Yeshua (Jesus) is the central figure in history and in the law, prophets, psalms (Luke 24:44) as well as the Gospels, Acts of the Apostles, apostolic epistles/scriptures, and book of Revelation.

Yeshua was God robbed in human flesh when he was on earth (John 1:14; 1st Timothy 3:16) and a descendant of King David (Psalm 11:1) and the Son of God simultaneously (Matthew 22:41-45). Yeshua is from the tribe of Judah (Revelation 5:5) and is the seed of the promise (Galatians 3:16). He is the great I AM (John 8:58) as well as a tried stone (Isaiah 28:1), the son of man (Ezekiel 2:11; 13:2), the righteous Branch (Jeremiah 33:15), the desire of all nations (Haggai 2:7), and the Lamb of God (John 1:29).

Yeshua is our liberator (Isaiah 61:1-4) and a doctor ("healer") who practiced medicine without a medical license (Acts 10:38). Jesus performed miracles (Mark 1:30-31) and is the only person in the history of the world as far as I know who defied the laws of gravity (Mark 4:37-41).

4

A Snap Shot into the Ministry of Yeshua Messiah of Nazareth

- To fulfill all things (Luke 24:44)
- To die (Deuteronomy 21:22-23)
- To be lifted up (John 3:14-16)
- To be beaten (Isaiah 50:4-7)
- To be unrecognizable (Isaiah 52:14)
- To be wounded (Zechariah 13:6)
- To be forsaken (Psalm 22:1)
- To please His Father (Psalm 40:6-8)
- To be despised and rejected (Isaiah 53:3)
- To be the Pascal Lamb (John 1:29,36)
- To seek (Matthew 18:11)
- To save his people from their sins (Matthew 1:21)
- To save sinners (1st Timothy 1:15)
- To bare our sins in his body on a tree (1st Peters 2:24)
- To be the faithful and true witness (Revelation 3:14)

Yeshua' relationship with the apostles

- The One who trained and sent them out to evangelize the-then known world (Matthew 28:19);
- The One who warned them about tribulations to come (John 16:33); and
- The One who supplied ALL of their needs (Philippians 4:19).

Yeshua' relationship with the church

- Is our mediator (1st Timothy 2:15)
- Is our great high priest (Hebrews 4:14-16)
- Is our deliver (2nd Timothy 4:18)
- Is our Comforter (John 14:18)
- Is our guide (1st Thessalonians 3:11)
- Is our Savior (Titus 2:13)
- Is our shepherd (John 10:11)
- Is our provider (Philippians 4:19)

Yeshua' role in the end times

- To send the Holy Ghost down from heaven (1st Peter 1:12)
- To endue believers with power (Luke 24:49)
- To be our Comforter (John 14:18)
- To be our Guide (1st Thessalonians 3:11)
- To be our Intercessor (Hebrews 7:25)
- To come back on the clouds (Acts 1:7)
- To separate the sheep from the goats (Matthew 25:32)
- To be King of kings and Lords of lords (1st Timothy 6:15)
- To deliver believers from wrath to come (1st Thessalonians 1:10)
- To deliver up the kingdom to his Father (1st Corinthians 15:24)
- To keep us from falling (Jude 23)

Yeshua' relationship with sinners

- To seek and save (Luke 19:10)
- To bring sinners to godly sorrow and repentance (2nd Corinthians 7:10)
- To rain on the unjust (Matthew 5:45)
- To snatch sinners out of hell fire (Jude 22)

Summary

Yeshua was God robbed in human flesh on earth, an evangelist (iterant preacher), teacher, healer, and the merciful and faithful high priest (Hebrews 2:17). Yeshua is our Apostle (Hebrews 3:1), a believer's example and role model (John 13:15), the Great Shepherd (Hebrews 13:20) as well as the Guardian of our souls (1st Peter 2:25, NLT; NASB). Above all, Yeshua is the Savior of the world and the coming King.

Thought

How has Yeshua (Jesus Christ) of Nazareth changed and touched your life?

Chapter 1, Section 3
A Snapshot into the Ministry of Saul of Tarsus, the apostle Paul

Introduction

About Saul of Tarsus

The apostle Paul is "a" key figure in the apostolic epistles and in the primitive Jerusalem and primitive Antioch churches.

Saul hated the "church of the living God" (1st Timothy 3:15) and wanted to destroy it by any means necessary (see Acts 7:56; 8:1-3). The Lord, however, stopped him in his tracks and used Saul to turn the-then world upside down (Williams, 2011, p.88).

Saul was not one of the twelve (Acts 1:13) and did not replace Judas Iscariot after he killed himself (Acts 1:20-22) nor James when he was beheaded (Acts 12:1-2). Saul was the son ("descendant) of a Pharisee (Acts 23:6) and according to (Bruce, 1980, p.44) a "pupil of Pharisees".

A Snap Shot into the Ministry of Saul of Tarsus

- To be a chosen vessel to suffer for his names' sake (Acts 9:15-16)
- To be a catalyst of social change
- To testify to what he had seen and heard (Acts 22:15; 26:16; Romans 1:1)
- To fulfill the will of God for the Gentiles (Acts 26:18)
- To be a faithful preacher, teacher, and apostle to the Gentiles (1st Timothy 1:12; 2:7)
- To share ALL the counsel of God (Acts 20:27)
- "To fulfill the word of God" (Colossians 1:25)
- To make known the mystery (Colossians 1:25-27; 2:9)
- To operate in the fruit (Galatians 5:22-23)
- To operate in gifts of the Spirit (1st Corinthians chapters 12-14)
- To be a witness (martyr) for the name of Jesus of Nazareth (Acts 23:11)

Summary

Saul of Tarsus (Paul) was not one of the twelve apostles, and he did NOT replace Judas Iscariot or James. Saul wanted to destroy the fledging church of the living God (1st Timothy 3:15) but could not (Acts 8:3; Galatians 1:13, 23; 1st Timothy 1:12). The Lord stopped him in his tracks and used Saul to turn the then-world upside down (Williams, 2011, p.88.).

Thought

What do you like and dislike about the epistles of Saul/ Paul?

CHAPTER 2

How Jesus Chose, Trained, and Commissioned the Twelve,
Saul of Tarsus, and Barnabas

Chapter 2, Section 1
How Jesus Chose, Trained, and Commissioned the Twelve

Introduction

Jesus of Nazareth did not beg, plead, trick, or twist anyone's arm to become one of his disciples. Jesus did not make, pay, or run anyone down to become one of his disciples. He just called (invited) men and left it up to them to follow him. Jesus had more than 12 disciples but only twelve apostles. In Chapter 2, section 1, I will talk about how Jesus chose, trained, and commissioned twelve men to become apostles.

Choosing the Twelve

Jesus chose the twelve apostles from among his disciples after he prayed all night (Luke 6:12-13). Of the 12, Jesus had a "chief" apostle and three personal confidants (Galatians 2:9; Mark 9:2-10). I also believe Jesus

<u>chose</u> the twelve "before the foundation of the world" (Ephesians 1:4) to fulfill scripture (Jeremiah 16:16) and in obedience to his Father. Jesus told the 12 approximately four times that he had chosen them (John 6:70; 13:18; 15:16, 19).

Training the Twelve

The twelve spent every waking moment of the day with Jesus. They heard Jesus teach in the temple court (John 18:20), in the synagogue (Luke 4:18; John 18:20), by the seashore (Mark 4:1-2), as they walked along the way (Matthew 12:1-4), and in private (Matthew 13:1-37).

Everything that Jesus said and did was a "teaching moment." Jesus taught the "twelve" everything that his Father had taught him (Isaiah 54:13; John 6:45), using the Socratic Method (Matthew 16:13-16) and a combination of whole, small group, and individual instruction.

Commissioning the Twelve

The phrase "the great commission" is not in the gospels. Before Yeshua ascended, he ordered the eleven to preach and teach the gospel to every creature under heaven and to make disciples, baptize and teach all nations [what he had taught them] according to Matthew 28:19 and Mark 16:15 respectively. Yeshua told the eleven to preach repentance and remission of sins in his name according to Luke 24:47 and to remain in the Jerusalem until they were endued with power from on high (see Acts 1:4)

Summary

Jesus Christ of Nazareth chose, trained, and sent the apostles into the then-known world to preach and teach the gospel to ever creature under heaven. Jesus taught the twelve what his Father had taught him. Jesus made the apostles fishers of men.

Thought

The Father sent the Son into the world to make disciples (twelve of which became apostles) and die for our sins. Before the Son ascended, he (Jesus) sent the eleven into the then-known world to preach and teach the gospel to every creature under heaven and to make disciples among all nations. Jesus chose the twelve, but the 12 did not choose him!

Chapter 2, Section 2
How God Chose, Trained and Commissioned Saul of Tarsus

Introduction

Saul of Tarsus appears in Dr. Luke's history of the church in connection with the death of Stephen (Acts 8:1). Saul hated the church (Acts 8:1-2). Why he hated the church is a mystery. To use our vernacular, Saul was a "bounty hunter" because he looked for believers to capture and imprison (Acts 8:3; 9:1-2). Saul was NOT one the twelve but was called to be an apostle while he was in his mother's womb. In Chapter 2, section 2, I talk about how God chose, trained, and commission Saul/Paul of Tarsus.

Choosing Saul/Paul of Tarsus

Like the prophet Jeremiah, God <u>chose</u> Saul to preach the gospel while he was in his mother's womb (see Jeremiah 1:5; Galatians 1:15-16).

Training Saul/Paul of Tarsus

Relative to training, Saul was NOT a disciple of Yeshua and was NOT trained by him but attended the synagogue and/or temple school for boys (Tenney, 1961, pp.99-100). Paul learned Torah, Mishna, and Talmud in the temple school (Tenney, 1961, p. 100) and received the gospel of Jesus Christ by revelation (Galatians 1:11-12). I believe God took what Saul learned in the synagogue and/or temple school and used it for his glory.

Commissioning Saul/Paul of Tarsus

God put Saul into the ministry at the height of his rage against the church of God (1st Timothy 1:12; Acts 9:1-5, 21). Unlike the prophet Jonah, Saul accepted his call and immediately began preaching the gospel (Jonah 1:3; Acts 9:25). In regards to his commission, God commissioned Saul when he was in Damascus through [the hands of] Ananias (Acts 9:10-19; 26:12-19).

Summary

God called Saul to be an apostle to "gentile" nations and used him to turn the then-world upside down.

Thought

God dealt with Paul in revelations and visions, but how does God deal with you?

Chapter 2, Section 3
How God Chose, Trained, and Commissioned and Barnabas

About Barnabas

Barnabas was NOT one of the twelve but was a leader in the primitive Antioch church before Saul (Paul) was converted (Acts 13:1-2). Barnabas was an unselfish man and was thus called the son of consolation (Acts 4:35-37).

I believe that Barnabas was:
- a disciple who did not walk away from Jesus of Nazareth (John 6:60, 66);
- one of the seventy special messengers (Luke 10:1-20; Boyle, 1990, p.43);
- a person who heard Jesus preach and teach the word (Mark 6:34); and
- a disciple who was scattered abroad following the death of Stephen (Acts 8:1).

The Lord put Barnabas and Saul of Tarsus into the ministry and used Barnabas to vouch (e.g. advocate, speak on the behalf of) for Saul (Acts 9:26-28) when they went up to Jerusalem by helping the brethren to fully understand that Saul had seen the Lord and was now one of them (Acts 9:27).

Introduction

The Acts of the Apostles is tacit (silent) as to who chose, trained, and commissioned Barnabas. I believe that Barnabas was chosen, trained, and commissioned by Yeshua to be an apostle. The "when-of-it" is anyone's guess!

Choosing Barnabas

I believe God <u>chose</u> Barnabas to be an apostle (Acts 14:14) to the gentile nations before the foundation of the world (Ephesians 1:4).

Training Barnabas

I believe Barnabas was a disciple who was <u>trained</u> by Jesus Christ of Nazareth but have no biblical proof.

Commissioning Barnabas

I believe the leaders in the church in Antioch (Acts 13:1-2) commissioned Barnabas and Saul when they sent them out on a special assignment by the Holy Ghost.

Summary

Barnabas was not one of the 12 but was an apostle nonetheless. God chose Barnabas to be an apostle before the foundation of the world.

Thought

Paul and Barnabas disagreed at times but did not let their difference interfere with their relationship and ability to win souls (see Acts 15:36-41; Proverbs 11:30).

CHAPTER 3

On The Dangers of Disobedience

Introduction

In chapter 4, I talk about obedience but before doing so will spent some time talking about the dangers of disobedience.

Disobeying the Lord Yeshua has grave consequences. For instance, disobedience caused Adam and Eve to fall into sin and die (Genesis 2:16-17).

Advantages associated with disobedience

There are, however, some advantages (at times) associated with disobeying man but not the Lord. For instance, the Egyptian midwives ignored the king's edit and did not kill Hebrew boys at birth. God in turn blessed the midwives to have their own children (Exodus 1:15-21).

The apostles were told under the threat of death not to mention and preach in the name of the Lord Jesus Christ but kept preaching the word (Acts 3; 4; 5; 12:1-2; 16:16-25). God allowed Saul of Tarsus to persecute the primitive church in Jerusalem but that did not stop the apostles and disciples from preaching the word of God (Acts 8:4; 11:19-21).

In the history of early America, it was against the law for anyone to teach a slave or freeman (black person) how to read and/or write. *"I will be heard!" Abolitionism in America* at website: http://rmc.the.library.cornell.edu/abolitionism/narratives.htm notes that "in most southern states, anyone caught teaching a slave to read would be fined, imprisoned, or whipped" (para.1).

Slaves Are Prohibited to Read and Write by Law found at website: http://www.historyisaweapon.com/defcon1/slaveprohibit.html indicate that in the early nineteen hundreds, the general assembly of the state of North Carolina passed a law which punished any white person or slave who taught a slave how to read or write. A white person who taught a slave how to read was fined but a slave who taught a slave how to read was whipped (para.2). Despite unjust laws, black people in America still learned how to read and write.

A few people in scripture who disobeyed the Lord and suffered as a result of it:

Ask Adam and Eve. Adam ate from the tree of good and evil and was evicted from the Garden of Eden with his wife (Genesis 2:16-17).

Ask Cain. Cain got angry and killed his brother Abel (Genesis 4:3-15).

Ask Lot's wife. Lot's wife turned into a pillar of salt because she just had to look back (Genesis 19:17-19).

Ask Moses. Moses died before his time because he got caught up into his emotions (Numbers 20:7-17).

Ask Samson. Samson lost his vision and died before his time because he played around with the devil (Judges 16:16-31).

Ask a kingless Israel. The nation of Israel was in and out of bondage because she did whatever she wanted to do whenever she wanted to do it (Judges 17:6; 21:25).

Ask King Saul. Saul was rejected as king of Israel because he did not kill the Amalekites (1st Samuel 15:1-26).

Ask King David. David could not build a house for the Lord because he had the blood on his hands (1st Chronicles 28:3), including Uriah's (1st Samuel 11:1-27).

Ask King Solomon. Solomon disobeyed the Lord when he intermarried and as such caused the kingdom of Israel to split (Deuteronomy 7:1-4; 1st Kings 11:1-13).

Ask a certain prophet. A certain prophet from Judah was mauled to death by a lion because he let the devil trick him into doing what the Lord told him not to do (1st Kings 13:1-34).

Ask the church in Galatia. The church in Galatia was in danger of being alienated from the Lord Jesus and would have fallen from grace if the brothers would have submitted to the teaching of certain men from Judea and got circumcised (see Acts 15:1; Galatians 5:1-4).

Summary

From Adam to the church at Galatia, disobedience has grave consequences. For instance, Adam was put from out of the garden (Genesis 3:23) and Lot's wife was turned in a pillar of salt (Genesis 19:26). Disobedience caused sin to come into the world through Adam (Romans 5:12), a judge to loss his sight, a king to be rejected by God, a kingdom to split, people to die before their time, a prophet to be mauled to death by a lion, and a church to fall from grace.

Thought

The devil "rebelled" against the Lord and was thrown out of heaven into the earth with his angels. I cannot, however, find a scripture which says that the devil disobeyed the Lord

—(Isaiah 14:12-17; Ezekiel 28:12-19; Revelation 12:7-9).—Have you?

CHAPTER 4

Obeying the Lord God

Introduction

Yeshua (Jesus Christ) of Nazareth and Saul of Tarsus play a powerful role in the history of the world. Jesus is the Savior of the world, whereas Saul was a sinner saved by grace who became the apostle to gentile nations. Yeshua did not come into the world with his own agenda but to please and do the will of his Father (Psalms 40:6-8; Hebrews 10:5-9).

God wants "all nations, kindred, people, and tongues" (Rev. 7:9) to obey Him. When "all nations, kindred, people, and tongues" obey the Lord, God will be pleased and bless us according to his will and purpose in the earth.

Several people in scripture obeyed the Lord and are in what I call *"The Obedience Hall of Fame:"*

- Enoch did not taste death and was translated because he pleased God (Genesis 5:21-24; Hebrews 11:5).
- Noah built an ark and saved himself and his household (Genesis chapters 6 through 8; Hebrews 11:7; 1st Peter 3:20-21; and 2nd Peter 2:5).

- Noah and his sons after the great flood were fruitful, multiplied, and replenished the-then earth (Genesis 9; Hebrews 11:7).
- Abram left his father's house, his country, and his relatives when he was seventy-five years old (Genesis 12:1).
- Abraham willingly offered up his only son (Isaac) as a living sacrifice (Genesis 22:1-14).
- Hagar went back to Sarah's house and thus submitted herself to Sarah (Genesis 16:9).
- Lot and his two daughters left Sodom and Gomorrah without looking back (Genesis 19:26).
- *Moses left the lap-of-luxury and suffered with the people of God (Hebrews 11:25).*
- Out of reverence to God, the sons ("descendants") of Levi did NOT worship the golden calf (Exodus 32:26-28).
- *Yeshua died for our sins according to the scriptures (1st Corinthians 15:3).*
- *Yeshua learned obedience through the things which he suffered (Hebrews 5:8).*
- The apostles and disciples preached the gospel under the threat of death (John 16:2; Acts 8:1-4).
- The lame jumped up on his feet and walked (Acts 3:1-9).
- Ananias went to Straight Street and laid hands on Saul of Tarsus and baptized him (Acts 9:10-17).
- The disciples did not let the great persecution following the death of Stephen stop them from preaching the gospel in the then-known world (Acts 8:1-4; 11:29).

- Philip went to Samaria and Gaza and ministered unto them (Acts 8:1-8; 26-40.
- Cornelius sent a delegation to Joppa to ask for Peter (Acts 10:1-9).
- Peter left Joppa and went to Caesarea (Acts 10:19-20).
- Saul of Tarsus accepted his ministry to Gentile nations (Acts 9:11-17; 22:4-12; 26:1-23).
- Out of obedience to God, children obey and are subject to their parents (Ephesians 6:1-3).

People who obey the Lord will:

- receive the gift of the Holy Ghost (Acts 5:32);
- be called a good and faithful servant (Matthew 25:21);
- inherit the kingdom (Matthew 25:34);
- receive of the Lord (1st John 3:22);
- reap material and spiritual benefits (Psalm 103:1-3);
- experience Jesus as the author of eternal salvation (Hebrews 5:9); and
- be counted as sheep (Matthew 25:31-40).

Summary

God wants "all nations, kindred, people, and tongues" (Rev. 7:9) to obey Him. It pleases God and puts a smile on His face when we obey Him.

Obedience will move us to behave a certain way. For instance, out of obedience, Jesus died for our sins according to the scriptures and was obedient until death (1st Corinthians 15:3; Philippians 2:8). Children will obey their parents (Exodus 20:12), a husband will love his wife (Colossians 3:19), a wife will submit to her husband (Colossians 3:18), and believers will obey the law (Titus 3:1).

Thought

Is it easier to obey God or man?

CHAPTER 5

The Principles of the Doctrine of Christ

Introduction

In the KJV, Hebrews 6:1 declares "to leave the principles of the doctrine of Christ and [to] go on to perfection" but Phillips renders, "Let us leave behind the elementary teaching about Christ and go forward to adult understanding." The question is: "What are the principles of the doctrine of Christ, and how do we go on to perfection?" The "principles of the doctrine of Christ" are standards of living that God has established for his people. For instance, God is "holy" and calls his people to be holy (Leviticus 11:44; 20:26). Thus, "holiness is a way of life, NOT a denomination"(Williams, 2011, p.167).

In this passage, the writer rebuked a group of (Jewish) believers who were too spiritually immature to teach others [unbelievers] the principles of the doctrines of Christ but instead needed someone to reteach them the elementary teaching (ABCs) of the gospel. The Hebrew writer wants his audience to grow up spiritually. A person can only go on to spiritual maturity when God allows it to happen. The six principles of the doctrine of Christ will be our focus of discussion.

Principle # 1: Repentance from dead works

"In those days came John the Baptizer preaching in the wilderness of Judah. He said: Turn to repentance for the kingdom of heaven is about to come" (Matthew 3:1-2, Howard).

Repentance

People everywhere need "to fear God and keep his commandments" (Ecclesiastes 12:3) and repent. "God wants genuine repentance, not lip service" (Halley, 1965). People need to repent from:
- whatever God hates (Proverbs 6:16-19);
- whatever defiles a man [living soul] (Matthew 15:17-20); and from the
- works of the flesh (Galatians 5:19-21)

To repent means to have a "change of heart and life wrought by the Spirit of God" (Vincent, 1888, p. 116). Repentance must be sincere and come from the heart (Isaiah 29:13). The scriptures declare that Godly sorrow brings a person to repentance and in line with the will of God (2nd Corinthians 7:10; 2nd Peter 3:9). People repent when they turn from their wicked ways (2nd Chronicles 7:14) and from darkness to light (Acts 26:18). Without exception, God "calls" men everywhere to repent (Acts 17:20).

Dead works

"Now the works of the flesh are evident which are adultery, fornication, uncleanness, lewdness, idolatry, sorcery, hatred, contentions, jealousies, outbursts of wrath, selfish ambitions, dissensions, heresies, envy, murders, drunkenness, revelries, and the like" (Galatians 5:19, NKJV).

The Hebrew writer talks about but did not define dead works. Dead works are of human origin and have the potential to destroy you.

Repentance from dead works

"I tell you, no; unless you repent, you will all perish as they did" (Luke 13:3, Moffatt).

God gives his creation a chance to repent from whatever he hates, whatever defiles a man, and from the works of the flesh (dead works) but cannot make us do it. If we, however, do not repent the "Father of lights" (James 1:17) will correct us like a good father (Proverbs 3:11-12).

Principle # 2: Faith towards God

"So Jesus answered and said to them, 'Have faith in God' "(Mark 11:22, NKJV).

Defining Faith

Jesus taught the apostles to have faith in God, not in themselves (Matthew 15:22-28).

Our faith must be in God not in a denomination, an economic, educational, or political system. Our faith must be in God alone!

You cannot buy faith from a fine department store, a boutique, a grocery store, off of e-Bay, or from a bargain store. "Faith is the substance of things hoped for and the evidence of things not seen" (Hebrews 11:6) and [faith] comes by hearing the word of God (Romans 10:17). Faith is:

- a fruit of the Spirit (Galatians 5:22-23);
- a gift of the Spirit (1ˢᵗ Corinthians 12:9); and
- a shield and source of protection (Ephesians 6:16).

Faith is essential in the life of a believer and thus cannot be bought, sold, or stolen. Faith starts small and grows (Matthew 17:20; Mark 9:23; Luke 17:6). In order to be saved and please God, people need faith (Ephesians 2:8; Hebrew 11:6).

Principle # 3: Teaching on ceremonial washings, ritual baths and the mikveh

"And Elisha sent a message to him saying, 'Go wash in the Jordan seven times, and your flesh shall be restored to you, and you shall be cleaned'" (2ⁿᵈ Kings 5:10, NKJV)

Introduction

Not all Bible translations say "of the doctrine of baptism." For instance the ESV and NAB assert, "...of the instructions of washing." Williams utters, "...of teaching about ceremonial washings," whereas Stern declare, "...and instructions about washing." The key element is that water is used in a ritual bath. When the Hebrew writer wrote about the doctrine of baptism, he did not write about the believer's baptism as noted in Acts 2:38 but about ritual and/ or ceremonial baths, which did NOT save anyone.

Pools and Mikvehs

There were pools in Jerusalem during the life and time of Yeshua of Nazareth such as the Pool of Bethesda and the Pool of Siloam. It is possible that those two pools were used as ritual baths. For instance, when Yeshua anointed the blind man's eyes with clay, he told him to go and wash in the Pool of Siloam (John 9:6, 11, 15).

Before General Titus destroyed the Temple in Jerusalem in 70 A.D. (Josephus, The Wars of the Jews 6.8.5, p.748), a mikveh was used by both Jewish men and women in order to obtain ritual purification (para.1) according to Wenger's (2009) article **Mikveh** at website http://jwa.org.encyclopedia/article/mikveh. The mikveh bath transformed a person from a state of ritual impurity to a state of ritual purity (para.2), just like being baptized in the name of Jesus Christ washes away a person's sins (Acts 2:38).

In her article ***Rising from the ritual bath*** at website http://www.ritualwell.original/rising-ritual-bath, Rabbi Jill Hammer notes that a mikvek is "a gathering of water" (para.1) which has been used by gentiles who converted to Judaism. For gentiles who converted to Judaism, the mikvek bath "is in effect, a rebirth ceremony" (para.3).

Others reasons to take a ceremonial and/ or ritual bath in a mikveh

- After contact with a dead person (Numbers 19:14-19)
- After childbirth (Leviticus [Lev.] 12)
- After a discharge (Leviticus [Lev.]. 15:16)
- Before being consecrated (Lev. 8).
- After menstruation (Lev. 15)

- Before the Passover (2nd Chronicles 29:34; 30:17; John 11:55)
- On the Day of Atonement (Lev.16)

Thought

The ritual bath made a person ceremonially fit but did not wash away anyone's sins.

Introduction

So far, I briefly talked about ritual baths in a mikvek but will spend some time talking about the believer's baptism. Know that God ordained the rituals baths ("washings") and baptism, not any religious group or denomination.

In-fighting and Baptism

Several denominations baptize in what some call the triune formula (titles) and say during baptism: "I therefore baptize you in the name of the Father, Son, and Holy Ghost" (Matthew 28:19). No matter what you say during a baptism, someone is going to criticize you for that. For instance, if you baptize in the name of the Father, Son and Holy Ghost and say being interpreted in the name of the Lord Jesus Christ, someone is going to criticize you for that. If you baptize in the name of Jesus, someone is going to criticize you for that. If you baptize in the name of Jesus Christ, someone is going to criticize you for that. If you baptize in the name of the Lord Jesus, someone is going to criticize you for that. If you baptize in the name of Jesus Christ into the change of God, someone is going to criticize you for that. If you baptize in the ha-Shem

(YHWH), someone is going to criticize you for that. If you baptize in the name of Yeshua Messiah, someone is going to criticize you for that. If you baptize someone in the name of Yeshua, someone is going to criticize you for that. If you baptize in the name of Jehovah, Jesus, and the Holy Ghost, someone is going to criticize you for that. No matter what you say conducting a baptism, someone is going to criticize you for that.

Baptism represents:

- a part of the new birth (John 3:1-5);
- participating in the death, burial, and resurrection of Jesus Christ (Romans 3:3-6);
- being buried with Christ (Colossians 2:11-13); and
- putting on Christ (Galatians 3:27-29).

Baptism after Israel came out of Egypt

God baptized Israel in the cloud when she passed through the Red Sea (1st Corinthians 10:1-2).

Baptism before the Ascension of Christ

Before the ascension of Christ, self-immersion was a common practice in the ancient world (Matthew 3:11; Mark 1:8). It is believed that John the Baptizer is the first person in the history of the world to baptize other people in water according Stegemann (1998), followed by the apostles under the tutelage of Yeshua (John 4:1-2).

Baptism after the Ascension of Christ

"Then Peter said unto them, Repent, and be baptized every one of you in the name of Jesus Christ for the remission of sins, and ye shall receive the gift of the Holy Ghost" (Acts 2:38).

The first mass baptism after the ascension of Christ is recorded in Acts 2:37-41. About three thousand souls were <u>added</u> to the fledgling primitive Jerusalem church. There were, however, other baptisms as recorded in the Acts of the Apostles.

- Philip baptized the Samaritans and the Ethiopian eunuch (Acts 8:12-16, 36-39);
- Ananias (who was a "disciple") baptized Saul of Tarsus (Acts 9:10-19);
- Peter baptized the house of Cornelius (Acts 10:47-49); and
- Paul baptized 12 certain disciples (Acts 19:1-6), Lydia and her household (Acts 16:14-15), the prison keeper and his family (Acts 16:27-33), and Crispus, Gaius, and the household of Stephanas (1st Corinthians 1:14-16).

Ritual Baths after the Ascension of Yeshua

I believe people took ritual baths in a mikveh after the ascension of Yeshua:

- Jewish people before participating in the first Pentecost celebration ("Feast of Weeks") after the ascension of Yeshua.
- Priests in Jerusalem who were obedient to the faith (Acts 6:7) in keeping with the Law of Moses.

- Certain men from Judea (Acts 15:1) and of the sect of the Pharisees who believed (Acts 15:5) in keeping with Law of Moses, customs, and traditions of the elders.
- Saul/Paul took a group of men into the temple to take a ritual bath and almost lost his life (Acts 21:17-33).

Thought

Baptism is essential in the life of a believer (Mark 16:16; Acts 2:38).

Principle # 4: The laying on of hands

"So he [Yeshua] could do no miracle there, other than lay his hands on a few sick people and heal them" (Mark 6:5).

Introduction

To lay hands on someone was a common practice in the ancient world and was not done hastily (1st Timothy 5:22). The laying on of hands was "a ceremony symbolizing identification and transfer in the OT" according to Unger (1967, p.758).

Laying on of hands

A person can lay hands on and bless and heal another person. For instance, Jesus touched babies, children and infants and blessed them (Matthew 19:13; Mark 10:13; Luke 18:15). Moreover, Jesus laid hands on a woman who was "bent double" and healed her (Luke 13:11-13).

Jesus had healing hands and healed others. For instance, when he touched Peter' mother-in-law' hand, the fever walked away from her (Matthew 8:14-15). Moreover, Jesus gave all believers the power to lay hands on the sick and heal them (Mark 16:16).

Receiving the Holy Ghost

A few people in scripture received the Holy Ghost after someone laid hands on them. The Samaritans received the Holy Ghost after Peter and John laid hands on them (Acts 8:14-19), whereas "12 certain disciples" received the Holy Ghost after Paul laid hands on them (Acts 19:1-6).

Sanctified for service

A person can be sanctified (set apart) to serve the Lord after someone lays hands on him or her. For instance, God used Moses to lay hands on Joshua to sanctify him to lead Israel into the promise land (Numbers 27:15-23).

A personal note

God still heals through the laying on of hands (Mark 16). For instance, in 1972, a certain pastor in a church in Newark, New Jersey poured oil on my mother's right leg, prayed, and the Lord healed her. A certain elect lady and evangelist in a church in Newark, New Jersey frequently laid hands on the sick and God healed them.

Other reasons for the laying on of hands

- To release a ministry in a person (1st Timothy 4:14)
- To bless a person (Genesis 27:27)
- To sanctify a person and/or tribe before the Lord (Numbers 8:9-11)
- To adopt children and bless them (Genesis 48:16)
- To transfer one's spirit (Numbers 34:9)
- To sanctify (set aside, designate) people for a work of ministry (Acts 6:16)
- To sanctify and send people off (Acts 13:1-3, JNT)

Thought

Do you believe that God can heal you through the laying on of hands?

Principle # 5: Resurrection of the dead

"And as it is appointed unto men once to die, but after this the judgment" (Hebrews 9:27, KJV).

Introduction

I do not believe that all men [living souls] will taste the sting of death, not unless it is the Lord's will that that person dies ("return to the dust of the earth"). Death came into the world by Adam but the resurrection [of life] by Jesus Christ (1st Corinthians 15:21). To resurrect means to bring something back to life that died physically. Jesus is the resurrection, and the life (John 11:25); and the first fruit of the resurrection (1st Corinthians 15:23).

A little proof

There is some evidence in scripture that a few people died and was resuscitated (brought back to life). For instance, after the resurrection Christ but before his ascension, godly men and women left their graves and walked the streets of Jerusalem (Matthew 27:51-53).

Under the law, two women lost a son who was brought back to life by faith (Hebrews 11:35).

- The Zarephath woman's son (1st Kings 17:9-11, 17-23); and
- The Shunammite woman's son (2nd Kings 4:18-21, 32-35).

During his earthy ministry, Jesus resuscitated three people:

- Jairus' twelve year old daughter (Luke 8:41, 49-55);
- a young man being carried to burial (Luke 7:12-15); and
- Lazarus of Bethany (John 11:38-44).

After the ascension of Christ, two people came back to life by the power of God (Matthew 10:8):

- Tabitha/Dorcas (Acts 9:36-42); and
- A young man in Eutychus (Acts 20:9-13).

Jesus and the resurrection

Jesus laid down his life (John 10:17-18) and spent three days and three nights in the heart of the earth (Matthew 12: 40). Jesus died on a tree (Deuteronomy 21:22-23) but is alive in heavenly places making intercession for his people (Hebrews 7:25).

The resurrection and the law

Job (Job 19:26), David (Psalm 16:10), Daniel (Daniel 12:2), Yeshua (John 6:40)), and Martha (John 11:24) believed in the resurrection of the dead. The Pharisees also believed in the resurrection of the dead but the Sadducees rejected it (Matthew 23:23-24). According to *The [Complete] Works of Josephus* (Josephus, Antiquities of the Jews, 18.1.3), "they [the Pharisees] also believe that souls have an immortal vigor in them, and that under the earth there will be rewards and punishments, according to as they have lived virtuously or viciously in this life; and the latter are to detained in an everlasting prison but that the former shall have to revive and live again" (p.477).

Thought

Embrace and be ready for the resurrection of the just to come.

Principle # 6: Eternal Judgment

"For the time is come that judgment must first begin at the house of God; and if it [judgment] first begin at us, what shall the end be of them that obey not the gospel of God" (1st Peter 4:17)?

Introduction

Eternal judgment is real and no one can bribe, buy, cheat, lie, or talk him- or herself from out of it. Once eternal judgement is rendered, there is no appeal process! A belief in eternal judgment can be found in scripture and in the Nicene, Athanasian, and the Apostle's creeds (The Dictionary of Biblical Literacy, 1989).

A belief in eternal judgment can be found in one of the prophets (Daniel 12:2). On a day designated by God, Jesus will separate all nations like a shepherd separates the sheep from the goats (Matthew 25:32). The sheep will be placed on his right hand (believers), whereas the goats (unbelievers) on his left hand (Matthew 25:33). On a day appointed by God, the 12 apostles will judge the 12 tribes of Israel (Matthew 19:27-28), the saints will judge the world and angels (1st Corinthians 6:2-3), and God will judge fornicators and adulterers (Hebrews 13:4, JNT).

Thought

The scripture says, "For God shall bring every work into judgment, with every secret thing, whether it be good, or whether it be evil" (Ecclesiastes 12:14). Eternal judgment is real and inescapable!

Summary

The Hebrew writer rebuked Jewish believers who needed to be "retaught" the principles of the doctrine of Christ when they should be teaching others [sinners] the ABCs of the gospel.

Repentance must be sincere and come from the heart (Isaiah 29:13). "God wants true repentance, not lip service" (Halley, 1962).

· We cannot buy, sale, or steal faith. Faith is a fruit of the Spirit, a gift, and a shield and source of protection. Above all, we are saved by faith through grace and cannot please God without it.

Taking a ritual bath is one of the principles of the doctrine of Christ and during antiquity made a person ceremonially fit to participate in the Feast of Unleavened Bread (John 11:55). In regards to baptism, John baptized the common people unto repentance for the remission of sins but after the ascension of Jesus, the apostles and disciples baptized for the remission of sin (Acts 2:38).

God can use all believers to lay hands on the sick and heal them. Moreover, a person can receive the precious gift of the Holy Ghost and be sanctified to serve the Lord in ministry through the laying on of hands.

There is proof of a resurrection of the dead in the Old Testament, the Gospels, and Acts of the Apostles.

The final judgement is real and unavoidable. Anyone's name that is not found written in the book of life will be the cast into the lake of fire (Revelation 20:15). No ands, ifs, or buts!

CHAPTER 6

On Why Believers Need the Holy Ghost

"But ye shall receive power, after that the Holy Ghost is come upon you" (Acts 1:8).

Introduction

God told the house of Israel that He would sanctify, sprinkle her with water, give her a new heart, and would put His spirit inside of her (Jeremiah 36:22-36).

God poured out His Spirit on the prophets, John the Baptizer, Elizabeth, Zacharias, Jesus of Nazareth, the apostles, the disciples, and on anyone who will obey him (1st Peter 1:11; Luke 1:15, 41-43, 67; 4:1; Acts 2:1-4; 5:32).

The Holy Ghost is the power from on high, the promise of the Father, another Comforter, a Teacher, a Guide, a Reminder, God, and the Spirit of Christ and God (Luke 24:49; Acts 1:8; Proverbs 1:23; Joel 2:28-32; Acts 2:38; John chapters 14 through 16; Romans 8:9; 2nd Peter 1:21).

The Holy Ghost does not discriminate along racial, ethnic, and gender lines and is not limited to any one particular group of people as God pours out his Spirit on ALL flesh (Joel 2:28). No one can buy the Holy Ghost from a fine department store, exchange, or steal it.

Needing the gift of the Holy Ghost

There are reasons as to why believers need the Holy Ghost. Jesus had the Holy Ghost and we need what he had. Believers need the Holy Ghost in order to be guided into all truth and shown things to come. Believers need the Holy Ghost in order to join the family of God (Romans 8:9), bear fruit (John 15:8), preach the word of God with boldness (Acts 4:29-31), walk in the spirit (Galatians 5:16, 25), and operate in the gifts of the spirit (Romans 12:3-8; 1st Corinthians 12:7-11).

A believer needs the Holy Ghost in order:

- to complete the new birth (John 3:5);
- to receive the **promise** of the Father (Luke 24:49); and
- to be endued with power from on high (Acts 1:8).

Summary

There are reasons as to why believers need the Holy Ghost. Jesus had it and we need never thing that he had in order to be anointed to serve Him. The Holy Ghost **cannot** be brought (Acts 8:9-24) and is the gift (Acts 2:38). In my way of looking at the world, the Holy Ghost is the gift-of-gifts and is also the good and perfect gift (James 1:17).

Thought

I pray that you receive the Holy Ghost.

CHAPTER 7

On Healing and Building a Fence around the Torah

Introduction

"Heal me, O Lord, and I shall be healed; save me, and I shall be saved; for thou art my praise" (Jeremiah 17:14).

Medical doctors "treat" physical illnesses but God is the only one who can heal as indicated in the scripture, "...for I am the Lord that healeth thee" (Exodus 15:26). There is a time to heal (Ecclesiastes 3:1-3; Psalm 103:2, 3) but God decides when to heal.

Healing

Jesus healed people during his earthly ministry without the aid of medicine (Acts 10:38) when he spoke the word and healed the centurion's beloved servant (Matthew 8:5-13), the Canaanite woman's daughter (Matthew 15:21-28), and the woman with the issue of blood (Luke 8:43-48). Some people were healed just by touching Jesus (Matthew 14:36).

Jesus healed a man with a withered hand, a woman with a spirit of infirmity, and a man with dropsy on the Sabbath (Luke 6:6-8). The Pharisees who witnessed the healings attacked Jesus when they asked him, "Is lawful to heal on the Sabbath day" (Matthew 12:10-13)? Jesus did not answer the Pharisees' question but instead asked them, "Is it lawful to do well on the Sabbath days or to do evil? to save life, or to kill" (Mark 3:4). The Pharisees did not answer Jesus' question or say a word. On another occasion, Jesus healed a woman with a spirit of infirmity on the Sabbath. The ruler of the synagogue who witnessed the healing retorted, "There are six days in which men ought to work (Leviticus 23:3): in them therefore come and be healed, and not on the Sabbath" (Luke 13:11-16).

The fence around Torah

God gave Israel and the stranger within her gates a day of rest (Exodus 20:8-11). God told Israel and the stranger within her gates not to work on the Sabbath (Deuteronomy 5:12-14) but did not say (operationalize) what work was. According to Numbers chapter 15, verses 32 through 36, a man was caught picking up sticks on the Sabbath and was brought before Moses for judgment. The man caught picking up sticks was locked up until God told Moses what to do. God handed down a death sentence and the man caught picking up sticks was stoned to death.

To keep Israel from sinning, the rabbis "built a fence around the Torah." According to website http://www.jewsfaq.org/halakhah.htm, the fence "is a law instituted by the rabbis to prevent people from accidently violating a Torah mitzvah." Halakkah: Jewish Law at website: http://www.mechon-mamre.org/jewfaw/halakhah.htm notes that "a gezeirah [fence] is a law instituted by the *rabbis* to prevent people from accidentally violating Torah" (para.12). In the minds of the Pharisees and ruler of the synagogue, healing on the Sabbath was work (Leviticus 23:3) and [Jesus] violated the fence(s) that the rabbis had built around the Sabbath.

One of the key points in *Building a Fence* at http://www.emethatorah.com/blog/2014/april-18/building-fences is that "the rabbis promoted the establishment of fences to protect the authority of Scripture" (para.10) but according to website http://heartofgodisrael.org/messianic-messagers/discipleship-is-jewish/ "The fence around the Torah is manmade commandments that made the instructions of the Torah burdensome" (para.11).

Building a fence around Torah is NOT limited to Judaism. The Hebrew scripture says not to kill and/or commit murder (Exodus 20:13). Thus, a denomination or religious group may build a fence around Exodus 20:13 and ask its adherents not to bear arms or join the armed forces.

Jesus and the fences

Jesus was not impressed at all with the "fences around the Torah" but instead was troubled by them. Jesus called the fences around Torah the commandments of men (Mark 7:1-13) and rebuked the Pharisees for replacing the word of God with their manmade traditions.

Unlike the rabbis and sages, Jesus appears to have built a fence around the Torah with scriptures. For instance, the commandment says not to commit adultery (Exo.20:14) and covet thy neighbor's wife (Exo.20:17). According to Jesus' teaching in Matthew 5:27-28, Jesus built a fence around the Torah with scripture when he taught that adultery does not just begin with the physical act but in a person's heart.

The people were taught to love their neighbors and to hate their enemy (Matthew 5:43). Torah does say to love one's neighbor (Leviticus 18:18) but not to hate one's enemy. The scripture declares, "Thou shall not hate thy brother in thine heart" and "not to bear a grudge against the children of thy people" (Leviticus 18:17-18). Jesus tore down the rabbis' fence around Torah when he taught the multitudes to love their enemies and people who did not love them (Matthew 5:43-48).

Summary

Medical doctors treat but do not heal anyone. God heals the human family through Yeshua of Nazareth (Isaiah 53:5). Moreover, the rabbis and sages may have built a fence around Torah with good intentions (?). Yeshua, however, was turned off by their fence(s) as the "fence" made the commandments of God useless.

Thought

I am healed by the wounds in his (Jesus') precious side (Isaiah 53:5).

CHAPTER 8

On What a Disciple Is

Introduction

The roots of discipleship can be traced back to the men of the great assembly who took steps to make sure that Israel did not go back into exile by being diligent in justice, building a fence around the Torah, and raising up disciples according to *Discipleship is Jewish* at website http://heartofgodisrael.org/messianic (paragraphs 8 –12).

The word "disciple" appears 29 times in the KJV, whereas "disciples" appears 243 times as stated in *How many times does the word disciple appears in the bible* found at website http://www.answers.com/Q/How many times does the word disciple appears in the b...

Disciples appear for the first time in the KJV in Isaiah 8:6, where it says "Bind up the testimony, seal the law among my <u>disciples</u>." Moreover, according to the *Thayer's Greek Lexicon* at website http://biblehub.com/greek/3101.htm, "the word [disciple] is not fond in the O.T., nor in the Epistles of the N.T." *Thayer's Greek Lexicon* (also) notes that "in a wide sense, in the Gospels, those among the Jews who favored him [Jesus], joined his party, [and] became his adherents." "Discipleship is an institution designed by Jews and passed down by Jews" as recorded in website http://www.jewsfaq.org/halakhah.htm.

On defining disciple

Disciple is a transliteration of mathetes, which is a learner, disciple, [and] pupil who has "the mental effort needed to think something through" as reported by website http://biblehub.com/greek/3101.htm. Bible scholars have defined "disciple" in several ways. The Strong's Concordance at website http://biblehub.com/greek/3101.htm defines disciple as "a follower of Christ who learns the doctrines of scripture and the lifestyle they require."

The online article *Disciple in the Bible* in Easton's 1897 Bible Dictionary at website http://dictionary.reference.com/cite.html?qh=disciple@ia=easton indicate that "a disciple are principally the followers of Christ who (1) believes in his doctrine, (2) rests on his sacrifice, (3) imbibes his spirit, and (4) imitates his example."

Disciple at website http://dictionary.reference.com/browse/disciple defines a disciple as "one of the 12 personal followers [apostles] of Christ, (2) one of the 70 followers sent forth by Christ, and (3) any other professed follower of Christ."

The definition of disciple as defined by *Merriam-Webster* at website http://www.merriam-webster.com/dictionary/disciple is "someone who accepts and helps to spread the teaching of a famous person..."In *Becoming a disciple of Yeshua* at website http://www.diggingwithdarrem.com/blog/2011/11/30/beoming-a-dis "a disciple is a life-long student of his rabbi (para. 5)" and "a fruit producing tree (para.16)." *Naves Topical Bible* (1974) indicates that a disciple is a follower of any teacher.

In my worldview, a disciple is a person under "spiritual" construction who is being conformed (transformed) in the image of his [dear] son (Romans 8:29), but as Dake's (1961) notes, a disciple is one who bears witness and speaks for Jesus and a believer in the church of Christ (*Smith's Bible Dictionary*, n.d., p.77).

The ultimate disciple

Jesus Christ of Nazareth was trained by his Father and did not attend the rabbinical and/or synagogue school of his day but despite his lack formal training was a prolific preacher and teacher (John 7:14, 15). Jesus was trained by the best and is the ultimate disciple.

Imperatives of a disciple

In *King of the Jews*, the author (as cited in website http:// heartof godisrael.org/messianic) talks about "the four main imperatives of a disciple" which are to
- "memorize their teacher's words;
- learn their teacher's traditions and interpretations;
- to simulate their teacher's actions; and
- to raise up disciples" (paragraphs 21-28).

A few points about the disciples of Jesus of Nazareth

The disciples (apostles) of Jesus ate what he ate, sat were he sat, and walked where he walked (Matthew 9: 10-11). When Jesus walked into the synagogue and into the Temple, the disciples walked in with him. When Jesus ate fish and bread, they ate fish and bread. Moreover, when the apostles needed something, Jesus supplied their need.

The disciples preached the gospel. When the primitive church in Jerusalem was scattered abroad following the death of Stephen (Acts 8:1-3), the disciples went everywhere and preached the gospel (Acts 11:19). No doubt, women preached too.

Attributes of a disciple

I believe that a would-be disciple should have certain characteristics. For instance, a would-be disciple with the help of the Lord should be docile (trainable), obedient, entrepreneurial (willing to take risk), able to follow directions, leadable, and pliable.

Choosing, selecting and the cost discipleship

Jesus chose chose the apostles after he prayed all night according to Luke 6:12-16 but during the first century, however, a would-be disciple approached a teacher-to-be of the law and asked him, "May I follow you?" The would-be disciple asked the teacher-to-be, "Do I have what it takes to be like you?" The would-be Torah teacher either accepted or rejected the disciple-to-be according to (http://followtherabbi.com/journey/issues). There were, however, a few rabbis who tried to recruit their own students (http://followtherabbi/guide/detail/r...).

Becoming a disciple during the first century was a highly selective process jjust as it is to get into professional and graduate school today in the United States because everyone who applies for admission will not qualify (make-the-cut) for admittance. For instance, Jesus called people to follow him but some did not accept his offer because they were unwilling to let their earthly possessions go to follow Jesus (Mark 10:17-22).

According to Matthew 16:24, a disciple-to-be had to:

- deny himself;
- take up his cross; and
- follow Jesus.

The cost of discipleship was high.

A first century disciple-to-be left everything that he had and abandoned his life as he knew it. For instance, when Jesus called Simon, Andrew, James and John, they left their fishing business (occupation) and families (Matthew 4:18-22). Moreover, when Jesus called Matthew (Levi), he left his job as a tax collector and followed Jesus (Matthew 9:9). The cost of discipleship then and now will cost you everything that you hold near and dear to your heart (Mark 3:13-19; Luke 6:13-19).

Disciple-teacher relationship

First century disciples spent all of their time with their teacher and developed a close emotional bond with him (http://heartofgodisrael.org/messianic-messagers/discipleship-is-jewish). Because of the close emotional bond, a father-son relationship emerged. The teacher became his students' father and the students became their teacher's sons. The disciple-teacher relationship transcended (went beyond) that of a father and son—a father brought his son into this world, but the sage would take him into the world to come as reported in *Discipleship in Judaism* by Rabbi Stan Farr (para.18).

Discipleship and women

Cyrus Adler and Lewis N. Dembitz report in their online article *Minyan* at website http://www.jewishenclopedia. com/articles/10865-minyan that women were not counted among the "quorum" of ten (men) necessary for public worship (para.1). In ancient Israel, women did not have to recite the daily Shema (Deuteronomy 6:4) or come to any feasts or festivals, and were not allowed to read from the Torah ("book of instructions") in the synagogue as reported in *Jewish women and the temple* at website http://www.bible-history.com/court-of-women/ women.html (para.4).

Some rabbis did not think too much of women as indicated in *The role of women* at website http://www. jewfaq.org/women.htm. The rabbis (at least some) believed that "women were lazy, jealous, vain and glut-tonous, prone to gossip and particularly prone to the occult and witchcraft" (para.9).

The sages and rabbis took men under their wings (arms) and turned them into disciples (para.15) but excluded women as potential students as indicated at website http://heartofgodisrael.org/messianic. Unlike the rabbis and sages, Jesus did not exclude women from discipleship. Women "followed" Jesus (Matthew 27:55) and listened to him preach and teach in the synagogue and temple. Women followed Jesus but "could NOT be disciples of any great rabbi or travel with any rabbi" as recorded in *Jewish women in the temple* (para.5).

Summary

Bible scholars have defined "disciple" in several ways. For instance, a disciple is a learner, disciple, [and] pupil who has "the mental effort needed to think something through" according to website http://biblehub.com/greek/3101.htm as well as one of the personal followers of Jesus, primarily the twelve. Thus "a disciple of Rabbi Jesus is one who totally surrenders to Him and His way of seeing and doing things (para. 13)" as reported in *Being a First-Century Disciple* at website https://bible.org/article/being-first-century-disciple. In my world-view, a disciple is a person under spiritual construction who is in the process of conforming into the image of Jesus of Nazareth.

Thought

A disciple [in the 21st century] should have certain characteristics and must be willing to abandon his life as he or she knows it in order to follow Rabbi Jesus.

CHAPTER 9

Purely by Chance

I became a part of the Shepherding movement purely by chance in 1981 after I was born again of the water and spirit. To say the least, I never heard of the Shepherding movement and it was Greek to me!

I was invited to a service at a church in a certain state purely by chance by a late dear friend. I attended the church for approximately one month before I was saved from my sins sitting in one of the church's services on Monday, July 20, 1981.

Then, I continued to attend services at said church on a regular basis purely by chance and was assigned to a shepherd by our then-pastor. At that juncture in my believer's journey, getting assigned to a shepherd was a good thing for me. I was a babe in Christ (1st Corinthians 3:1) and needed guidance. Unlike first century would-be disciples, I did not look for a shepherd. I heard my shepherd preach a few times at a gospel service purely by chance but never heard-of or knew anything about him.

Entering into a shepherd-sheep relationship was not all peaches-and-cream. I, nonetheless, enjoyed the fellowship with my shepherd and his family. The brother was a good Bible teacher, an awesome preacher, and a powerful praise and worship leader. I enjoyed listening to him sing and watching him and his wife dance before the Lord. I had a good shepherd and still respect him and his family.

My experience with the Shepherding movement, albeit brief, makes me wonder what did the apostles and disciples like and dislike about their interaction and relationship with Jesus of Nazareth. *Although Jesus was God robed in the flesh (John 1:1, 14), he was still a man.* I got involved in the Shepherding movement purely by chance but left by choice.

Summary

I got involved in the Shepherding movement purely by chance in 1981 but left by choice. I did not ask for or look for a shepherd but one was assigned to me.

Thought

Embrace the Lord who is "our" shepherd (Psalm 23:1).

CHAPTER 10

Some Things to Consider

1. Jesus Christ of Nazareth could not die for our sins according to the scriptures as a child (1st Corinthians 15:1-3).

2. Sin is kryptonite and is not your friend (Romans 6:23).

3. I cannot live with myself when I compromise who and want I am.

4. A college does not respect you at all when one of its operatives schedules you to teach courses without consulting with you first about your availability and the courses that you would like to teach.

5. A liar can and will use the truth against you.

6. "If we do not speak out, we will suffer the consequences of silence" (Williams, 2011, p.167).

7. The wages of sin is still death (Romans 6:23).

8. "My heart's desire and my prayer to God is" (Romans 10:1) for people who discriminate against others on the basis of age, race, ethnicity, nationality, disability, sexual orientation, sexual preference, marital status, gender-identity, religious ideology, political beliefs, and social and veteran status is that they might be saved.

9. "People are precious" (Williams, 2011, p.165).

10. Physicians and dentists are "among" the doctors but are NOT the only doctors!

11. If you think education is expensive, try ignorance or is it the other way around?

12. **Jesus still saves, hears, and answers every prayer.**

13. *I would like to hear about a local, state, and federal official during my lifetime who repented of his or her sins, got baptized in water in the name of the Lord Jesus Christ, received the precious gift of the Holy Ghost, spoke in tongues, walk in the Spirit, operate in the gifts of the Spirit, and praise the Lord in dance like King David!*

14. *The academic and/or scientific literature may help you live in this present world but what about the one to come?*

15. Embrace the Bishop Michael V. Robinson Rule — turn pages, find what you say in the book [Bible].

16. I cannot begin to understand for the life of me "why" some men sit in church with hats on their heads.

17. ***A father does not stop loving his son just because he plays with his emotions and tell him lies.***

18. A person can remove a Confederate Flag from a state office building but cannot remove the symbolism of the flag from a person's heart.

19. People talk about "doubting" Thomas as if he were the only one (John 20:20-25)!

20. *Beware of **emotional predators** which come to you in friends' clothing but are inwardly wolves.*

21. The food that we throw in the garbage in the United States can feed people who eat from out of the garbage.

22. "People make time to do what they want to do" (Williams, 2011, p.164).

23. A bully may be uneducated or educated, but what difference does it make!

24. Only the strong survive "when" and "where" they can.

25. *We may be related by blood but are family by relationships.*

26. Medicine helps but then creates its own problems.

27. Preach your "convictions" but do not shove them down my throat and punish me when I disagree with you.

28. ***I believe that ALL people are God's creation (Genesis 1:27) but not all people are his children (John 8:44; Romans 8:9)!***

29. "God is [still] able" (Williams, 2011, p.164).

30. The word of God is good in and for you.

31. ***I preach the gospel but cannot make you believe the gospel.***

32. *Take your own advice and see how it feels.*

33. God loves us but at the same time will turn around and correct us like a good father (Job 5:17).

34. I wonder whose ideal it was to charge airline passengers for snacks and to check-in luggage.

35. *I rather depend on the Lord than man (Psalm 118:8).*

36. *Getting baptized in the name of the Lord Jesus Christ is a part of what you need but not all of what you need (Acts 2:38)*.

37. I am saved from sin and the judgment to come.

38. *I am familiar with child abuse, elderly abuse, sexual abuse, spiritual, and spousal abuse but what about "friend" abuse?*

39. "There is no expiration date for prayer" (Williams, 2011, p.166).

40. **A predator does NOT care about its prey!**

41. *What are you like when you are alone?*

42. *What can you do and say without offending someone?*

43. *It is more blest to give than to be taken advantage of (Acts 20:35)*.

44. Watch as well as pray (Matthew 26:41).

45. *"I thank God for his grace and mercy" (Williams, 2011, p.166.)*.

Summary

In this section, I share with you from real life some things that I think are worthy of consideration. "Some Things to Consider" may open your eyes, bless you, encourage your precious soul, and at the same time make you mad!

Thought

What do you find worth considering and changing in your life?

REFERENCES

Birnbaum, P. (1998). Encyclopedia of Jewish concepts. Rockaway Beach, New York: Hebrew Publishing Company.

Boyle, I. (1990). The ecclesiastical history of Eusebius Pamphilus. Grand Rapids, Michigan: Baker Book House.

Bruce, F.F. (1977). Paul: Apostle of a heart set free. Grand Rapids, Michigan: William B. Eerdmans Publishing Company.

Edershem, A. (1994). Sketches of Jewish social life (updated edition). Peabody, Massachusetts: Hendrickson Publishers, Inc.

Freeman, J.M. (1996). Manners and customs of the bible. New Kensington, Pennsylvania: Whitaker House.

Halley, H.H. (1962). Halley's bible handbook: An abbreviated bible commentary (23rd edition). Grand Rapids, Michigan: Zondervan Publishing House.

Nave, O.J. (1974). Nave's topical Bible—A digest of the Holy Scriptures. (Rev. ed.). Chicago, Illinois: Moody Press.

Robertson, A.T. (2000). Word pictures in the New Testament concise edition (edited by James A. Swanson). Nashville, Tennessee: Holman Bible Publishers.

Smith, W. (n.d.). Smith's bible dictionary. (Rev. ed.). Nashville, Tennessee: Holman Bible Publishers.

Strong, J. (n. d.). The exhaustive concordance of the bible. Mclean, Virginia: MacDonald Publishing Company.

Tenney, M.C. (1861). New Testament survey. Grand Rapids, Michigan: Wm. B. Eerdmans Publishing Co.

The American heritage dictionary. (2rd edition). (1991). Boston, Massachusetts: Houghton Mifflin Company.

The Revell concise bible dictionary (1991). Tarrytown, New York: Fleming H. Revell Company.

The works of Josephus: New updated edition (1987). Peabody, Massachusetts: Henderickson Publishing, Incorporated (translated by William Whitson).

Vincent, M.R. (2nd ed.). (1888). Word studies of the New Testament. Peabody, Massachusetts: Hendrickson Publishers.

Vines, W.E., Unger, M.F., & White, W.J. (Eds.). (1985). Vine's expository dictionary of biblical words. Nashville, Tennessee: Thomas Nelson Publishers.

Williams, T. (2011). 2 in 1: Leaving something behind: A brief examination of text and A few bible-based poems and sayings. Fairfield, IA: 1st World Publishing.

www.ingramcontent.com/pod-product-compliance
Lightning Source LLC
LaVergne TN
LVHW091206080426
835509LV00006B/851